Anonymous

The Child and the Bishop

Anonymous

The Child and the Bishop

ISBN/EAN: 9783337146078

Printed in Europe, USA, Canada, Australia, Japan

Cover: Foto ©Lupo / pixelio.de

More available books at **www.hansebooks.com**

THE CHILD AND THE BISHOP
TOGETHER WITH
CERTAIN MEMORABILIA
OF
THE R^T REV PHILLIPS BROOKS DD
LATE BISHOP OF THE DIOCESE OF MASSACHUSETTS

BY
AN OLD FRIEND

BOSTON
J G CUPPLES & C^O
BOYLSTON AND CHURCH STS
1894

TO THE MEMORY OF

MARY ANN (PHILLIPS) BROOKS,

THE MOTHER OF A GREAT MAN.

CONTENTS.

PREFACE	ix
EXTRACT FROM LETTER OF BISHOP BROOKS	xiii
THE CHILD AND THE BISHOP	19
MEMORABILIA	
A CHAPTER FROM MEMORY	29
THE SERMON ON PRESIDENT LINCOLN	37
AS RECTOR IN PHILADELPHIA	43
PHILADELPHIA DIVINITY SCHOOL	47
CLERICUS CLUB	53
AS RECTOR IN BOSTON	59
AT HARVARD COLLEGE	63
TRAVELS	65
OUTSIDE LABORS	67
BOSTON REMINISCENCES	71
AS BISHOP	83
ESTIMATE	89
HISTORICAL PARALLEL	97
L'ENVOI	103

PREFACE.

A GREAT desire having been expressed by many people to possess the picture which appears as a frontispiece to this volume, it was thought best to place it in this little book, the copyright proceeds from the sale of which are devoted to the creation of

THE MARY CRESSON FUND
FOR
THE BOSTON HOME FOR INCURABLES

this charity having especially interested Bishop Brooks. The only public bequest made by him in his will was for this institution.

"Hear the words of the Gospel written by St. Mark in the Tenth Chapter, at the thirteenth verse : —

"They brought young children to Christ that He should touch them ; and his disciples rebuked those that brought them — but when Jesus saw it he was much displeased, and said unto them, Suffer the little children to come unto me, and forbid them not : for of such is the Kingdom of God. Verily, I say unto you, whosoever shall not receive the Kingdom of God as a little child, he shall not enter therein. And he took them up in His arms, put His hands upon them, and blessed them."

Service for the Baptism of Infants.

HUS saying he (Socrates) got up and went into another room, and Crito followed him: but us he requested to stay behind. We remained, therefore, talking over with one another and inquiring into what had been said: ever and again coming back to the misfortune that had befallen us: for we looked upon ourselves as doomed to go through the rest of life like orphans bereft of a father."

PLATO'S PHAEDO, 116.

EXTRACT FROM A LETTER.

INDEED I had a delightful visit. I still seem to hold 'Beautiful Blessing' in my happy arms. . . . I like to think of the new church getting more and more familiar every Sunday. It must never lose association with 'B. B.' and me, who gave it its first consecration. But how quickly it will lose its newness and get filled with memories.

Ever affectionately yours,

P. B.

Boston, May 23, 1890.

The Child and the Bishop.

THE CHILD AND THE BISHOP.

GIRT with those fast folded arms,
Safe, yet with tenderness pressed,
Calm is the innocent child,
Peaceful the trusting soul,
Quiet the nesting face,
As strength and innocence meet,
Spanning the perfect arch,
Twixt Man in completest power,
And Infancy's opening life!

Little one looking away,
Pulling the curtain aside,
Out of the windows of time,
Out from the Wakening Soul,
What is Thy vision of life?
Image of houses and men,
Playthings of creaturely joy,

THE CHILD AND THE BISHOP.

Flowers, and blossoms, and birds,
Life in its manifold forms, —
These are the objects thine eyes
View from the window's wide pane.

Tired Thou turnedst again,
To the arms which are holding Thee fast,
To the smile which enchains in its peace
The fluttering spirit within;
Calm, Thou beholdest once more
The eyes of the prophet of God
Casting their light into Thine!

And what in the face of the child,
Preacher of faith, seest Thou?
Helper and Bishop of souls,
Friend and Bringer of Hope,
Torch-bearer here in the dark
And cavernous chambers of doubt,
What dost Thou see in the soul,
What in the face of mankind,—
Looking far out upon time,

THE CHILD AND THE BISHOP.

Up through the windows of life,
What dost Thou see in us all?

We have grown weary, our walk
Trembling, and road-sore our feet;
Nothing of life can we solve,
As Thou, our leader and friend,
Dost the divineness of God
See in the children of men.

This dost Thou teach us, we know
This much Thy soul has made clear:
That the life is the light of mankind
(As the angels in Heaven behold
The face of the Father in light).
Never to falter in faith,
Never to sink into self,
Never to barter the gold
Of the Spirit for passable coin,
Not to play false to the soul,
This is Thy word to the world,
This is Thy message to men!

THE CHILD AND THE BISHOP.

And in thine eyes have we seen
The glow of the vision divine;
Under the smile of Thy soul,
Brother and Helper, have we
Caught from the light of Thy face
A life that the world cannot know;
Manhood, and duty, and faith,
Mastery over the flesh,
Triumph through patience and truth,
Light from the spirit of God,
Strength from the cross of our Lord,
This have we gathered from Thee!

Yes! from Thy grasp upon God,
The light of the mount on Thy face
Shining resplendent in life,
We, on the sands of the plain,
Glimpses of glory have seen;
Something of light and of fire,
Something of faith and of calm
From Thy presence among us have snatch'd.
Something have saved from the halt

THE CHILD AND THE BISHOP.

In the Caravan's March o'er the plain,
Where like the prophet of Old
Waiting in silence, alone,
Thou on the crest of the mount
Broughtest God's message to men.

Out of the windows of life,
Out of the caverns of doubt,
Forth on the welcoming world,
Close to the life of mankind,
Thou, like a Master of Souls,
Shewest the way for our feet!

Yes! and the Father's lost face,
Seen in the sons of mankind,
Ever Thy spirit hath shown!
Deep in the marshland of sin,
Faint in the darkness of night,
Straying like sheep that are lost,
Still in the heart of mankind,
The image of God in the soul,
'Twas thine to explore and reveal,
Brother and preacher, and friend.

THE CHILD AND THE BISHOP.

Thou for the sheep of Thy flock
Shepherd of Shepherds, and friend
Of those who in doubt and in fear
Their faith in the tempest have lost,
When darkness has swept o'er the soul
And the lights one by one have gone out,
The windows of Heaven have seen,
Hast pointed with finger of Hope
To the penciled light in the sky,
To the glow that cometh at eve,
The sureness and truth of God,
To those who will trust and obey!

The golden clouds of the west,
Seem not more truly the dust
Of the feet where our God is seen,
Than the Scaffolding Thou hast built,
Whereby in these toiling hours,
The soul can ascend to its God,
And finish the temple's wall,
That building not fashioned with hands,
The Spirit's Eternal abode!

THE CHILD AND THE BISHOP.

Dead Thou art not, O Man —
Dead Thou canst never be!
Not 'mid the graves of earth
Thy living voice shall we seek,
Thy loving soul shall we find!
Thou art to us as a star
Fixed in the quiet sky,
Seen in the silent hours,
Giving a light for all time,
Ruling the blackness of night,
Shining forever the same!
There art Thou poised, and the days
That move with invincible force,
Rapid, resistless and sure,
Never can hide from our eyes
The light and the joy of Thy soul,
Helper and Leader of men,
Bringer of peace and of light,
Witness to God and mankind!

Memorabilia.

A CHAPTER FROM MEMORY.

SOME time during the summer of 1858, the Rev. Phillips Brooks came to Philadelphia to be the rector of the Church of the Advent at Fifth and Buttonwood Streets.

His friend and fellow seminarian, the Rev. Henry A. Wise from Virginia, was then rector of the Church of the Saviour, West Philadelphia, and was electrifying great congregations who flocked to hear his swan-like discourses as with hectic face and trembling voice he went from church to church preaching by invitation on successive afternoons and evenings.

Phillips Brooks and Henry A. Wise came to the same field from the Virginia Seminary, though Wise was first on the ground

MEMORABILIA.

and had earned his following, when the shadow of death was seen in his face and the storm of the coming war of the rebellion was beginning to break. And so the way was left open for the young Bostonian who was at the little Church of the Advent at Fifth and Buttonwood Streets.

It was at first a question whether this so-called transcendental mind, would fit the average Philadelphian. But it is the sign of genius to fit the situation whatever that situation may be, and in three months' time, this young man whom his evangelical friends eyed askance and his High Church friends could not begin to fathom, was started at his bicycle gait, spinning his way straight up the heights to Olympus, while all the religious world wondered. This tall young man came one Sunday afternoon to preach for his friend, the rector of St. Paul's. It was the rector's custom in those days to invite the new clergymen who came to the city into his pulpit, and to welcome them with a few words of brotherly greeting. Great was the surprise of this visitor to find himself classed in a category which was utterly unknown and unfamiliar to him; a surprise which was shared by the large audience when the sermon was over, since they failed to recognize the sign language and test words of the evangelical vocabulary. The sermon was from the words, "Master, which is the great commandment of the law?" And when it was over something strange had happened to the inmates of a number of pews. A land which was dim and far off came very near; a shadowy glimpse of a future age which had been born of boyish dreams stood out as clear as a landscape, seen through a nicely adjusted field-glass, and it seemed as if the day for which

MEMORABILIA.

the young mind of that period was waiting had come.

After the service the young preacher came home to the father's house to supper and met the family.

But the preacher did not say very much to the boys. Something seemed to be the matter with his collar and the boys were rather shy of this strange and mysterious visitor, and so the morning and the evening of this friendship were the first day, and the party broke up after supper, when the host returned the favor, and went with his guest to preach at his little church on Fifth Street. And thus this great ministry and this lasting friendship began. After these days, when the young preacher was a power, throned like a king in the pulpit which had been built for his old friend and pastor, Alexander H. Vinton, and when the boys whose eyes, like those of Balaam, were opened, were now

MEMORABILIA.

in college looking forward to their own coming ministry, how many and how helpful were the hours stolen from routine duties, when, sitting by the door of the Church on Rittenhouse Square, they listened to the voice and drank in the full, deep inspiration of that nobly anointed nature. Many a Sunday afternoon, when the wide doors of that Church were thrown back, and the crowds flocked out into the open air, it seemed to those listeners coming out into the street again, as if the very heavens were on fire, not because the sun was setting across the Schuylkill, but because the preacher had projected a light into the open sky of the heavens; the light of the mystic, the light of the prophet; that light which never was on sea or land. Wordsworth says in his matchless Ode —

"Shades of the prison-house begin to close

Upon the growing boy;
But he beholds the light, and whence it flows,
He sees it in his joy.

At length the man perceives it die away,
And fade into the light of common day.

In those war days in Philadelphia great Union meetings were held in different churches and men forgot their religious differences in the fact that they were loyal to the government, or were the much hated "copperheads", a term of reproach taken from the reptile world, from the insidious habit of this serpent which lay low and bit the heel of those who passed by, a trait as old in history as the questionable blessing of the dying patriarch upon the tribe of Dan, when he said:

"Dan shall be a serpent by the way: an adder in the path, that biteth the horse-

MEMORABILIA.

heels so that his rider shall fall backward." (Gen. xlvii, 17.)

At many of those famous war meetings the young Bostonian was a most welcome speaker, and whether he offered prayer or spoke a word of cheer and counsel, his tall lithe form was ever a benediction.

THE SERMON ON PRESIDENT LINCOLN.

How wonderfully prophetic are the following passages taken from his funeral eulogy on Abraham Lincoln as the dead body of the martyred President lay in Independence Hall.

It was a marvellous address for one so young to make as far back as 1865. When one reads it now nearly thirty years later, and sees this outline eulogy realized and filled to the letter in the after career of Phillips Brooks, the words of the noble of Ethiopia come into the mind as after reading Isaiah's glowing page he said to Philip the Deacon by his side, "of whom speaketh the prophet thus, of himself or of some other man?" (Acts viii, 34.)

"The more we see of events the less we come to believe in any fate or destiny ex-

MEMORABILIA.

cept the destiny of character. It will be our duty then to see what there was in the character of our great President that created the history of his life, and at last produced the catastrophe of his cruel death.

"From his boyhood up he lived in direct and vigorous contact with men and things, and both his moral convictions and his intellectual opinions gathered from that contact a supreme degree of that character by which men knew him, that character which is the most distinctive possession of the best American nature, that almost indescribable quality which we call in general clearness or truth, and which appears in the physical structure as health, in the moral constitution as honesty, in the mental structure as sagacity, and in the region of active life as practicalness.

"A great many people have discussed very crudely whether Abraham Lincoln was an intellectual man or not : as if intellect were a thing always of the same sort, which you could precipitate from the other constituents of a man's nature and weigh by itself, and compare by pounds and ounces in this man with another. The fact is that in all the simplest characters the line between the mental and moral* natures is always vague and indistinct.

"They run together and in their best combinations you are unable to discriminate, in the wisdom which is their result, how much is moral and how much is intellectual. You are unable to tell whether in the wise acts and words which issue from such a life there is more of the righteousness which comes of a clear conscience or of the sagacity which comes of a clear brain.

"It is the great boon of such characters as Mr. Lincoln's that they reunite what God has joined together and man has put asunder. In him was vindicated the greatness of real goodness and the goodness of real greatness. The twain were one flesh.

"This union of the mental and moral into a life of admirable simplicity is what we most admire in children; but in them it is unsettled and unpractical. But when it is preserved into manhood, deepened into reliability and maturity, it is that glorified childlikeness, that high and reverend simplicity, which shames and baffles the most accomplished astuteness and is chosen by God to fill his purposes when he needs a ruler for his people, of faithful and true heart. Such as he had who was our President.

"Here then we have some conception of the man. Out of this character came the life which we admire and the death which we lament to-day. He was called in that character to that life and death. It was

MRMORABILIA.

just the nature . . which a new nation such as ours ought to produce."

These extracts taken from the discourse preached at the Church of the Holy Trinity while the body of the President was lying in the city, show us the unconscious prophecy and confession of Phillips Brooks' own rich and harmonious well-poised character, as after the nearly thirty years which have passed since this funeral oration was delivered, that character has produced an impression upon the Christian world unparalleled by any living man of this century.

MEMORABILIA.

AS RECTOR IN PHILADELPHIA.

He preached the Baccalaureate Sermon for the graduating class of 1865 at the University Chapel on Ninth Street, Philadelpia, the first time that this chapel was used for such a purpose. Those who remembered the famous "exhibitions" of the University of Pennsylvania with the jargon of comic programmes and rival and opposing claqueurs will not forget this occasion when, the Glee Club acting as choir, the young preacher, then in the rising glory of his greatness as the rector of Holy Trinity church, preached a sermon from the words, "The light of the body is the eye: if therefore thine eye be single thy whole body shall be full of light, but if thine eye be evil thy whole body shall be full of darkness. If therefore the light that is in thee be darkness, how

MEMORABILIA.

great is that darkness!" (Matthew vi, 22, 23.)

The young minister lived in those days at Locust and Sixteenth Streets; and at Spruce Street, No. 1339; and at 1,115 Walnut Street. His rooms were always most attractive: there was never the smell of the shop about them, but on the contrary always the delicious repose of the idler, the latest reviews and magazines, the newest books, the most fascinating pictures and bits of art, while the fragrance of tobacco lingered over the curtains, manuscript and bric-a-brac, and one never was in a hurry to leave.

The same delightful friendship which he formed for a few college men, and most carefully and persistently nurtured and cherished, continued when these collegians became seminarians at the Philadelphia Divinity School at Thirty-ninth and Walnut Streets, West Philadelphia.

MEMORABILIA.

His brother Frederick Brooks was at the Divinity School in those days, a thoughtful earnest quiet man, and three or four little groups or knots of men rallied around the personality of the younger Brooks, and that of a very remarkable young man of Scotch birth and ancestry who was easily the leader of all who came into touch with him, John Irving Forbes.

One of these seminarians on a certain occasion read an essay at the Divinity School which attracted the favoring judgment of this Agamemnon among the students, and into his room one night at 11.30 o'clock walked the Rev. Phillips Brooks, demanding without further parley or comment, but in an imperious and commanding way which was always his own distinctly effective way, that the essay in question should be forthwith immediately read.

The student in question, after vainly demurring and apologizing and explaining the matter, saw his big visitor settle himself down with a pipe to listen, his big eyes ogling the shy student out of a week's repose of mind, as he remarked: " Come, come now, it's late, go on, let me hear it, and remember I want to hear it not because Forbes believes in you fellows, but because you fellows believe so tremendously in Forbes. I always like men who believe terribly in other men."

MEMORABILIA.

PHILADELPHIA DIVINITY SCHOOL.

The origin of the Philadelphia Divinity School is like the sources of the Nile, and the beginning of all history, shrouded in myth and fable. There were men who graduated from this school before it was a school, and before the classes came into regular and apostolical succession, but they were like the men who lived before the flood or like the kings who reigned before the Pharaohs, or like the dragons of the period who lived before the gate was hung on its hinges in Eden. Their record on the page of history is precarious and uncertain. These aboriginal gentlemen of the early miocene period of the Divinity School used to meet in the basement of St. Luke's Church, where they were instructed by the early Professors of that rising institution. Dr. Howe, then

MEMORABILIA.

rector of the Church; Dr. May, who was imported from Virginia to be the main spring of this new enterprise; Dr. Stone, who was translated from Massachusetts to be the lecturer on evangelical theology; Dr. Vaughn, who was the George Herbert type of character, himself the lecturer and the model of what was termed "pastoral care," and Dr. Van Pelt whose title was the familiar one which in Hebrew means "teacher," together with Dr. Hare whose work at the Episcopal Academy was then over, were the early instructors of this dawning school of the prophets. The hands of that great organizer, Bishop Alonzo Potter, were seen under this institution, but it had to begin somewhere without money and without price, without the interest of the rich or the favor of those high in church affairs. So it began in the basement of St. Luke's Church, in Philadelphia, and the path which led to it was like the path the poet Watt describes in his psalms in metre:

"But wisdom shows a narrow path,
With here and there a traveller."

But there came a day when to airy nothingness there was given a local habitation and a name, and in the early years of the sixties, or just when the civil war was dawning, the Alibone mansion at Thirty-ninth and Walnut Streets, in West Philadelphia, with its large house and stable, received this migratory school of the prophets journeying westward according to Bishop Berkeley's prophetic advice, and there the school became a great power, and rested for a score of years until the present edifice with its spacious halls and chapel was erected.

John Irving Forbes was the great character of those days to all who knew him, and in many ways the most original and striking personality that the Philadelphia Divinity School ever produced. He died in 1871, three years after his graduation.

Forbes fairly made the men who clustered round him over again. He turned them inside out as the skilled farmer turns over to the sunlight, the damp wet hay. He dragged men out of their inner selves : taught them to think, and thrilled them with his own masterful leadership, and was a perfect Socrates to an admiring group who lived upon his bold and fearless ventures into the abyss of the unknown. Himself a mystic, an old Catholic, and a thorough-going Mauricean, the men who were about him were as clay in the hands of the potter. In those days he was in constant communication with Maurice, and used to read from time to time the wonderful letters sent to him by the great preacher and philosopher of Lincoln Inn's Fields. He was always in debate

MEMORABILIA.

with the professors, always respectful and reverential in manner, and always conservative in expression and profoundly radical in thought.

It was his interesting leadership at the Philadelphia Divinity School which so attracted the mind of the young preacher of Philadelphia to this group of willing eager disciples.

At the time of the ordination of these men, together with a venerable pastor of one of the city churches, the graduating class from the Philadelphia Divinity School (which was ordained in the year 1868) found themselves invited to a breakfast the day before their ordination at the celebrated Augustin's Restaurant in Philadelphia, where these embryo young clergymen were made the guests of their friend, the Rector of the Church of the Holy Trinity.

During these days, and for the few years

MEMORABILIA.

following, one by one this group melted away into the natural condition of married life. As one of these young men appeared for the sixth time at the chancel rail of the Church of the Holy Trinity in the capacity of groomsman, to meet the bridesmaid who was his companion at the chancel gates, the Rector, who had been officiating at the wedding, remarked in sotto voce, "How long, O Cataline, wilt thou abuse our patience?" to which the young man replied as he met his companion and walked down the aisle with her, "Positively my last appearance in this capacity."

MEMORABILIA.

CLERICUS CLUB.

It was such circumstances as these with an admiring group of young students which began this remarkable friendship. Later on, a few of these students at the Philadelphia Divinity School found themselves once more the circling companions of their illustrious friend, now, however, the scene of their activities being removed to Boston. It was in the year 1870 that the famous Clericus Club in Boston began, a club which had had its first innings, so to speak, in the city of Philadelphia in the year 1867. The following description of the beginning of this club is taken from the "Remembrances of Rev. Phillips Brooks" by Rev. Dr. C. A. L. Richards, page 34.

"What a host he was to us, the members of this club from which he is taken. It clus-

MEMORABILIA.

tered about him in the beginning, and he remained its loved and honored centre to the end. To most of us, however loyal to one another, its meetings have meant primarily an evening with Brooks. The first meeting, in the fall of 1870, was held at his rooms in the Hotel Kempton, not more than half-a-dozen of us being present. We were rather dull, perhaps, at that first meeting. Brooks often has reminded me how I lingered behind at the close and said, ' I wonder if this club will ever get together again.' As usual, he was hopeful, and his hope prevailed.

"We had no laws, and no officers but the secretary, who became the sole fountain of law. When we needed authority we appealed to him. It was understood that this club was limited to twenty. The agreement was useful as a point of departure. We never exceeded that number until we wanted more, when, a few founders protesting, more

MEMORABILIA.

came in and the club became twenty-five. That bound is final; no one would dream of passing it; so our present number of members is thirty-three. Our course has been absolutely consistent. We have had no law, and have disregarded any precedents that were likely to acquire the force of law. Brooks always acted as president, though no such office was known to exist among us. Time has a little impaired our original structure. We have a president and secretary now, and where the law-making power resides only constitutional adepts can determine.

"After his election to the Bishopric it seemed best to him to disarm prejudice by resigning his presidency in this club and accepting membership in other like societies. He was glad to be with them, but we cannot fail to remember, also, how his heart lost no interest in this club, how often he met with

MEMORABILIA.

us, how cordial he was with us. For many years our meetings were in his study. He would have it so, and it was pleasant to be his debtor for hospitality so gladly offered. He said, the last time I saw him, that if he had known how often he could arrange to be at home on club nights, he should have urged us to retain our old meeting place. Our 'loving cup' given him on his election to the Bishopric was a source of pride and pleasure to him, of greater pride and pleasure to us who gave it, in slight token of our love and gratitude. He took it as he took any such tribute, not at all as his due, but as if his friends were so good and kind to him."

The old Philadelphia Clericus Club always seemed to this transplanted group in Boston like the recollections of some earlier preexistent state, or like a trial trip of the steamer before the machinery was finally adjusted for the great voyage of life. Happy indeed are they who can look back upon this doubly cemented friendship, bound and riveted with the precious recollections of the life in Boston and the earlier days of preparation in the city of Philadelphia.

AS RECTOR IN BOSTON.

In the fall of 1869, just six weeks after he had furnished his study in the residence of his very dear friend, the Rev. Charles D. Cooper, in Philadelphia, the final summons came which compelled him to see that it was his duty to go to Boston. There he was found later on by the willing emigrants of Philadelphia who came to settle around him in the Hotel Kempton on Boylston Street, where the Boston Clericus Club was established, and later in Marlboro Street, and finally in the spacious rectory of Trinity Church on Clarendon Street.

This new house was to him a great delight, and great was his joy in furnishing it and in ordering it according to his cosmopolitan ideas of living. Certain rooms were known as Bishops' rooms, and five-dollar rooms and one-dollar rooms, and the old guests of Philadelphia days learned the lesson of the "Gospel Feast" and often, in mock humility of spirit, began, with shame, to take the lowest rooms, or in other words the choicest chambers.

One of these friends wrote him, after his election to the Bishopric, to the effect that he would not feel at home any more in the old rectory, fearing that he might meet the house of Bishops, like angels, ascending and descending upon the well known stairs, as these Bishops were often known as the "angels" of their different dioceses; to which the reply was, "Indeed, the diocesan angels did never take the place of those who have gone up and down Jacob's ladder all their life."

A certain clerical friend, stopping for a day or two at the house at the beginning of a six weeks' vacation, was tempted, day by

MEMORABILIA.

day, to remain for nearly a fortnight, in which time he met a number of distinguished English visitors who found the hospitality of this rectory as inviting as the aborigines had done.

Here were met, at different intervals, Canon Farrar on his visit to America, Rev. Mr. Haweis, the well known clerical musician, Bishop Anthony Thorold, formerly of Rochester, the present Lord Bishop of Winchester, and it was here that Dean Stanley, on his visit to America, found himself so welcomed and at home.

The Dean's visit to New England filled Dr. Brooks with great delight, and as the Dean himself had taken no greater pleasure than in showing American visitors the wonders and beauties of Westminster Abbey, so this courtesy was most gladly and cheerfully returned by his illustrious host in tak-

MEMORABILIA.

ing him to Cambridge, Salem, Plymouth and the region of the Berkshire Hills.

The bust which stands to-day in the alcove in Trinity Church is a perpetual survival of that glad visit of Arthur Penrhyn Stanley, bringing with him in his day of sorrow and cruel loss in the death of his beloved wife, the welcome and the blessing of the famous Abbey of London to the famous Trinity Church of Boston. Canon Farrar, Mr. Haweis and the Bishop of Winchester have all expressed, since the death of Bishop Brooks, their deep and tender gratitude for the many courtesies and favors shown them while visiting in America.

MEMORABILIA.

AT HARVARD COLLEGE.

The interest and devotion of Bishop Brooks for Harvard College was one of the most remarkable and interesting features of his life. Harvard never for one moment lost its interest in her illustrious son, and those who were guests at his house when he was doing service as Chaplain at Harvard, will well remember the early breakfast, perhaps eaten alone that the guests might not be disturbed, and the punctual horse and coupé at the door at an early hour to take him every day for six weeks to Appleton Chapel, that he might there open the service of the day and turn what might have been regarded by some as the unmeaning function of prayers into the beauty of a gracious and loving service. And who that has heard him preach in Appleton Chapel before that throng of

MEMORABILIA.

expectant students, can ever forget the marvellous way in which he planted himself, and the truths for which his life has always stood, deep into the moral nature of untold numbers of America's choicest youth? Is it any wonder that the last act in the pageant of his funeral was the passing of the procession through the uncovered ranks of Harvard's sons in the great open campus at Cambridge just before the body reached the gates at Mount Auburn?

TRAVELS.

Phillips Brooks was particularly fond of travelling and of mingling with life in all its varied forms. His visits abroad were many and interesting. The trips to all sorts of out of the way places, the visits to distinguished men, his sojourn with Tennyson at the Isle of Wight, his meeting with Gladstone and Browning in London, the interviews with missionaries and wise men in India were all recounted to his friends in the most delightsome manner, with the artlessness of a child and the simplicity of a maiden recounting her delight at the first ball.

When he returned to Boston, his friends of the clergy and laity gave him a dinner at the Hotel Brunswick to welcome him back, and those who heard him speak on this oc-

MEMORABILIA.

casion will well remember the conscious struggle that went on in his nature between his desire to make emphatic his appreciation of the compliment shown him on that occasion, and his equally strong desire to bring before the minds of the churchmen of the Western World the great lessons of moderation and simplicity and open-heartedness which it has been the mission of the East ever to impress upon the more active and mechanical life of the Western World. "Ah! Converse," he was heard to say as the meeting broke up, "how good, how very good it was in you and all these other brethren thus to welcome back such a wilful wanderer."

OUTSIDE LABORS.

Dr. Brooks was one of the early originators and promoters of the American Church Congress system and made it a special point to be always present at the meetings of its sessions. He followed its course with the deepest interest and was always one of its most helpful advisers and friends. The triennial General Convention of the Episcopal Church was less attractive to him as a matter of course, but it is an interesting phenomenon to watch the change in his attitude toward this law-making body. From being at first an outside critic, he grew to be a recognized debater in the lower house, and was always most courageous and chivalric in his admiration for and defence of men of conviction whose guiding beliefs led them to take

MEMORABILIA.

the floor in defence of their cherished articles of faith.

No words can express his oft repeated admiration for the skill and ability displayed by the Rev. Dr. Morgan Dix, the honored presiding officer of the House of Clerical and Lay Deputies, and it was this admiration for Dr. Dix which led Dr. Brooks to accept the invitation from the Rector of Trinity Church, New York, that he should hold a mission there in Lent for a certain week in each year. Those who were present at these preaching services in Trinity Church, New York, will not soon forget the scene there witnessed, with crowds of business men flocking into the sacred building from the busy environs of Wall Street, the simple and primitive service, the gracious host seated in the chancel, and the eloquent and

MEMORABILIA.

impassioned preacher giving his message to the business men of New York from that historic and impressive pulpit.

MEMORABILIA.

BOSTON REMINISCENCES.

The building of Trinity Church, Boston, its removal to the Back Bay in the face of much opposition, the erection of the church and chapel and the absolute freedom of the entire work from debt, was in itself an achievement for a lifetime. Yet, to those who looked on during these days of struggle between the brilliant Richardson and the average "practical" committee man (so-called), nothing was seen but perennial serenity of spirit in the life of this busy creative personality.

Everything was right, and all would come right, and so Richardson the architect, and La Farge the decorator, and Norcross the builder, each were happy in that freedom

MEMORABILIA.

which allowed them their own special way with the new church.

To a clustering group of elderly clergymen how loyal and tender this man was in his relationship! Dr. Stone, the venerable dean of the new Divinity School at Cambridge, was always treated with the love of a loyal affectionate son. So always was the mention of Dr. Sparrow's name at the Alexandria Seminary. To Dr. Vinton his former pastor at St. Paul's, Boston, and subsequently his admiring and retiring tutelary divinity in Philadelphia, Mr. Brooks was always the fond and devoted clansman and follower.

His funeral discourse on Dr. Vinton wherein he was eulogized as the great commoner, the great presbyter of the American Episcopal church, was the fit and touching tribute of a loyal life-long friend.

For Bishop Paddock, Dr. Brooks had as years grew on and he came to recognize the

MEMORABILIA.

soundness and wholesomeness of his influence in Massachusetts, nothing but words of praise.

And for clergymen of other folds, like Dr. Peabody and Dr. Gordon and the different pastors of the Boston pulpit, he had always kind and brotherly words as he applied to them the Master's words, "By their fruits ye shall know them."

He preached everywhere, and was the servant of all; now at the Young Men's Christian Union, now at Appleton Chapel, now at the Moody Tabernacle, and later at Trinity Church, New York. But the Lent Lectures at St. Paul's Church, Boston, were in a certain unique way his greatest occasions, and the mission and meaning of Lent never seemed so clear and real as when standing up with that vast concourse of business men one realized the far off words of the prophet, "How beautiful upon the mountains are the feet of them that preach the gospel of peace."

It was very seldom that Phillips Brooks talked about himself or his own personal experiences. He would tell to a few friends of Browning, or Gladstone, or Tennyson, or of his visit to the Queen, Windsor Castle, but always in such a way that the personal equation in the tale was reduced to the lowest possible terms.

His love of clear and simple humor was marked and emphatic, and he had a rippling way of describing ludicrous scenes which was like nothing so much as a bubbling gurgling brook laughing its way over rock and stone and moss.

There was a member of the Clericus Club who used to tell for him at stated intervals after the most importunate and irrepressible command, a long drawn yarn about an English showman, in which absurd description of men and scenes and animals and historic events always aroused his keenest laughter. When this story was repeated to him, he nearly always became aroused, left his chair, stirred the fire, put on more fuel, walked the floor, puffed at his cigar most vigorously, and ended by joining in the story, repeating stray snatches with a falling and rising cadence after the manner of the recital of a Greek chorus.

No one of the old set has heard that story since the day when he went away from his friends, and it would seem sacrilege to hear it ever again.

There was a sermon which he preached a number of times the year before he died, on the text "If I may apprehend that for which also I am apprehended of Jesus Christ," in which he analyzed most subtly and skillfully the power and meaning of a life-long friendship. It was nothing less than the con-

MEMORABILIA.

fession on his part of the great and abiding value which he placed on certain very intimate and tender associations with those who stood near to him and were dear to him.

Lover, husband, father, were relationships which were denied him. So he gathered the trailing vines of his heart's affections and wound them round his brothers who were his truest friends, and round his truest friends who were his brothers.

It was with him as Tennyson describes it in "In Memoriam:"

> "Thy voice is on the rolling air;
> I hear Thee where the waters run;
> Thou standest in the rising sun,
> And in the setting Thou art fair.
>
> "Far off Thou art, but ever nigh;
> I have Thee still, and I rejoice;
> I prosper, circled with Thy voice;
> I shall not lose Thee though I die."

MEMORABILIA.

As one reads over again the familiar pages of his Browning how underscored and emphatic certain passages become as illumined by the clear and spiritual life of Phillips Brooks!

During the first days of his absence from earth, as the minds of his friends tried to become accustomed to the hard strange thought of the grave, and the funeral and Mount Auburn, how the opening lines of La Saisiaz, again and again asserted themselves:

>"Good, to forgive;
>Best, to forget!
>Living, we fret;
>Dying we live.
>Fretless and free,
>Soul, clap thy pinion!
>Earth have dominion,
>Body, o'er thee!

MEMORABILIA.

"Wander at will,
 Day after day,—
 Wander away,
 Wandering still—
 Soul that canst soar!
 Body may slumber:
 Body shall cumber
 Soul-flight no more.

"Waft of Soul's wing!
 What lies above?
 Sunshine and Love,
 Skyblue and Spring,
 Body hides — where?
 Ferns of all feather,
 Mosses and heather,
 Yours be the care!"

And the following passages from Browning's early poem of "Pauline," seem to have become illuminated and made intensely

MEMORABILIA.

real by this nature which made men see what was meant by the "light of life:"

"So, as I grew, I rudely shaped my life
To my immediate wants; yet strong beneath
Was a vague sense of power though folded up,
A sense that though those shades and times
    were past,
Their spirit dwelt in me, with them should rule.
. . . .
"As life wanes, all its care and strife and toil
Seem strangely valueless — while the old trees
Which grew by our youth's home, the waving
    mass
Of climbing plants heavy with bloom and
    dew,
The morning swallows with their songs like
    words,
All these seem clear and only worth our
    thoughts:
So aught connected with my early life,
My rude songs or my wild imaginings,

MEMORABILIA.

How I look on them — most distinct amid
The fever and the stir of after years !

. . . .

"And one star left his peers and came with
peace
Upon a storm, and all eyes pined for him;
And one isle harbored a sea-beaten ship,
And the crew wandered in its bowers and
plucked
Its fruits and gave up all their hopes of
home ;
And one dream came to a pale poet's sleep,
And he said, 'I am singled out by God,
No sin must touch me.' Words are wild and
weak,
But what they would express is, — Leave me
not,

. . . .

Be still to me
A help to music's mystery which mind fails
To fathom, its solution, no mere clue !"

MEMORABILIA.

As one remembers his preaching, or reads his sermons, or comes across the fragment of some of his letters, how strangely in his death the teachings of his life are made emphatic, according to the Master's words, "And now I have told you before it come to pass that when it is come to pass ye might believe."

He was so veritably in the spirit-world while all the time he was so thoroughly at home with his friends in the flesh that as one said recently, "I think of him as now here, and now there, flitting back and forth between heaven and earth so continually, that when I do not see or hear him here any more, I simply conclude that he is staying a little while longer on the other side."

AS BISHOP.

When he was very tired and worn after twenty years of incessant labor at Trinity Church, Boston, his friends perceived after his declination of the Philadelphia Bishopric and the Harvard College professorship, that the only way out from the Trinity Church routine was by electing him as Bishop Paddock's successor.

He was very coy and shy about it at first, but finally came to see that it was the one only thing for him to do, and so he consented to be nominated.

A friend who had watched the balloting on the day of the Convention and had counted ninety long ballots (which were the Brooks ballots) dropped into the box, grasped his hat and ran over to the Clarendon Street rectory full twenty-minutes

MEMORABILIA.

before the announcement was made, and found him with his niece in the spacious library. "Brooks, you are Bishop!" was the simple announcement. "How do you know?" was his answer, as he rose to pace up and down the apartment. "Because you have ninety clerical ballots and you only want seventy and the laity are all right. Come get ready, the Committee will be here soon to tell you that you are Bishop of Massachusetts. See, here comes Mr. Chester the sexton running, he has come to verify this statement!"

He paused a moment, and put down his cigar, pleased and flushed, and yet as quiet as a child with its promised gift, and then said, "Bishop of Massachusetts! well! you have chosen a queer bishop." And the callers came and the disciple that did outrun the sexton found himself constrained to come in a second time, along with the

MEMORABILIA.

formal committee, and solemnly and formally assist at the official announcement of the fact that had already so informally been made known.

But even then it was too late. The spirit was burning itself straight through the flesh and no power of man could turn the flight of this soul backward. Those who knew him best and saw him most, recognized a burning sense of impatience to be through with the mission of life, a bewildering expression of helplessness in storming any longer his hard way against the inevitable, and a strange sense of the closing in of the environment of his life in the clutch of destiny. There was a richness and roundedness of experience: there was a gentle, tender, inexpressible desire to be the servant of all men: there was a strangely subdued and chastened tone which made one think of the face of the Ecce Homo, the man of sorrows and acquainted with grief, in these last three years which caused his friends to realize as never before the jarring tactless questioning of the Sons of the Prophet at Bethel and at Jericho to Elisha, "Knowest thou that the Lord will take away thy Master from thy head today. And he said, Yea I know it: hold ye your peace!"

Trinity Church within three short years witnessed three great sights in the closing years of her beloved pastor's life. Those three great occasions were as follows:

Phillips Brooks' last day as the rector of the church, when he seemed to single into his farewell discourses all the teaching and preaching of the twenty years which had gone before; the day of his consecration as Bishop, when he seemed under that great dome to be harnessed and fastened into the Chariot service of the Lord God Almighty, like some mailed and armored angel; and the day of his funeral, when the great open Square in front of the church became the outer court for this service for which any Church must prove itself to be too small!

In these latter years he had gathered great wisdom: was always strong in his positions: acquired a sagacity which was a sort of running guide to his entire life and that of his companions, and had built himself over again in those points in his nature where the early seams of his limitations had been visible. His criticism faded away; an early indescribable Bostonian air melted into the larger atmosphere of social and religious cosmopolitanship; he grew to respect the men he once most bitterly opposed, and the perfect span of his catholicity was reached when Father Hall was welcomed into the Clericus Club, and when he took the ground that Father Grafton should not be disqualified from being Bishop of Fond-du-Lac, since if he was sound enough to be a presbyter in the Church, he was sound enough to be a bishop.

"If we refuse to consent to Grafton's election", he wrote, "we will help to keep the Episcopate forever narrower than it now is."

ESTIMATE.

Papers, reviews, and published pamphlets have all honored his name in the articles which have been written about him, and these with unnumbered sermons from pulpits throughout the English speaking world, have told the story of his life and have drawn the lessons which his character teaches.

The following extract from an editorial in the Philadelphia Press, condenses into a few striking sentences, that which others have taken many pages to elaborate:

"In the work, which Dr. Brooks discharged for a third of a century, he overtopped all his contemporaries who labored in this great harvest by his direct capacity to express spiritual conviction. In an age when there is a constant tendency to treat Christianity as a body of doctrine and dogma,

MEMORABILIA.

or as a code of ethics and conduct, as calling for belief in a creed or for a moral life, he grasped the greater truth that these are but parts and phases, manifestations and fruits, of the spiritual life revealed to the race at Bethlehem and on Calvary. It is the object and aim of the entire framework and structure of doctrinal and practical Christianity to impress upon men the reality and the sufficiency of this life, to place man in harmony with the divine, but in the anxiety of most preachers to impress and explain their explanation, they fail to carry home to their hearers the simple spiritual message of the Gospel.

"This can only be accomplished by a man in whom the conviction of spiritual things has been raised to that white heat in which all truth,— the message of revelation and nature, of science and religion, of creed and conduct,— can be welded into a flawless

MEMORABILIA.

whole. Much which is usually held indispensable to the orator on platforms, sacred or secular, was absent in Dr. Brooks. His swift, rapid and monotonous utterance, the want of relief and dramatic portraiture, a lack of systematic, ordered and logical argument,— this and much else prevented his sermons from leaving on mind or memory that impression of matchless and consummate art which has marked the greater pulpit orators of all ages, but these things were the merest trifles and must all be trifling by the side of the tremendous effect produced by the overmastering conviction of the realities of life and of its spiritual solution which Dr. Brooks impressed on all his hearers.

"Conviction breeds conviction. Earnestness induces earnestness. The effect which Dr. Brooks created and continued to create with every fresh appearance was rooted and

MEMORABILIA.

grounded in that grasp of things spiritual on which all human power of expression and interpretation ultimately rests For the wise and the foolish alike, this world is but an empty thing unless its passing show is lit with a spiritual significance. No man will lack for hearers or for influence over his fellow-men who is aflame with this conviction and whose assertion of it is constant and unhesitating. On this truth the power of all higher literature rests, and by it men are swayed as the wheat by the wind. To one to whom this is clear, the doubts and difficulties of the day disappear as they did for those who came under the power and influence of the spiritual conviction and belief of the great preacher just gone.

"His profound conviction of those spiritual certainties which underlie life and play their part in every attempt to explain its profounder significance enabled him, at a time

MEMORABILIA.

of great confusion in thought and great doubt over fundamental spiritual conceptions, to marshal those broad and far-reaching harmonies of the spiritual world which awake and respond only to the touch of genius of the highest order. He delivered an old message — no man more clearly or more faithfully — but he presented it in terms and forms which met modern needs and quelled modern doubts. For his church and his denomination, for the two cities in which he labored and in which his death is felt as a public loss, he did much; but he did yet more in quickening the religious life of the nation to a fresh confidence and conviction that the things of the spirit are still mighty to prevail over all else that darkens life like a cloud and robs the future of its brightest hope."

In his imagination and his spiritual transcendence over the routine methods of the

MEMORABILIA.

intellect, he was like Emerson: in his simple desire to get at directly spiritual returns for life, he was like Wesley: in the practical side of his life, he was like the English Cromwell or the American Cleveland. He was a genius without the infirmities of the temperament of genius, and his daimon or genius worked itself out on the field of religious activity. It might have taken the field of literature, society, business, politics or the bar or medicine, and have secured as hearty a recognition of its power as it did in the ministry. But there was a divine Providence in this life, and the call from God determined the field wherein this anointed nature was to exercise its powers, according to St. Paul's ascending climax or progression of character:

"For whom he did foreknow he also did predestinate. Moreover whom he did predestinate them he also called: and whom he called them he also justified; and whom he justified them he also glorified."

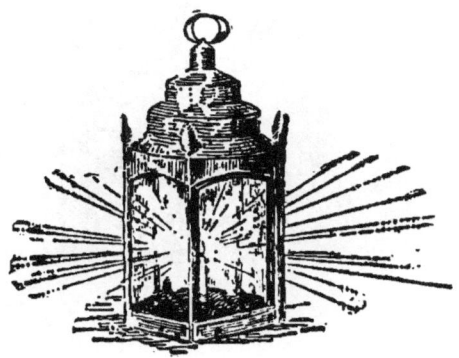

HISTORICAL PARALLEL.

Rev. Dr. Harwood, of New Haven, in his most interesting sketch of Bishop Brooks' character and career compares him in the hold of his personality over the populace and the shortness of his Episcopate to Arch-Bishop John Tillotson, in the reign of William and Mary.

The comparison is most striking and suggestive, and satisfies that innate feeling of the heart to localize in all history the place of our living favorites.

In view of the bitter opposition, the cruel "trial by scourging", through which the late Bishop Elect of Massachusetts passed, during the six months which preceded his consecration, all of which he passed in absolute silence, how striking in its similarity of experience is the following extract from Macaulay's History of England :

"Tillotson was nominated to the Archbishopric, and was consecrated on Whitsunday, in the church of St. Mary-le-Bow. Compton, cruelly mortified, refused to bear any part in the ceremony. His place was supplied by Mew, Bishop of Winchester, who was assisted by Burnet, Stillingfleet and Hough. The congregation was the most splendid that had been seen in any place of worship since the coronation. The Queen's drawing-room was, on that day, deserted. Most of the peers who were in town met in the morning at Bedford House, and went thence in procession to Cheapside. Norfolk, Caermarthen and Dorset were conspicuous in the throng.

"Devonshire, who was impatient to see his woods at Chatsworth in their summer beauty, had deferred his departure in order to mark his respect for Tillotson. The crowd which lined the streets greeted the new Primate warmly. For he had, during many years, preached in the city; and his eloquence, his probity, and the singular gentleness of his temper and manners, had made him the favorite of the Londoners. But the congratulations and applauses of his friends could not drown the roar of execration which the Jacobites set up.

"According to them, he was a thief who had not entered by the door, but had climbed over the fences. He was a hireling whose own the sheep were not, who had usurped the crook of the good shepherd and who might well be expected to leave the flock at the mercy of every wolf. He was an Arian, a Socinian, a Deist, an Atheist. He had cozened the world by fine phrases, and by a show of moral goodness; but he was in truth a far more dangerous enemy of the church than he could have been if he had openly proclaimed himself a disciple of Hobbes, and had lived as loosely as Wilmot.

"He had taught the fine gentlemen and ladies who admired his style, and who were constantly seen round his pulpit, that they might be very good Christians and yet might believe the account of the Fall in the book of Genesis as allegorical. Indeed they might easily be as good Christians as he; for he had never been christened; his parents were Anabaptists and he had lost their religion when he was a boy; and he had never found another.

"In ribald lampoons he was nicknamed Undipped John. The parish register of his baptism was produced in vain. His enemies still continued to complain that they had lived to see fathers of the Church who never were her children. They made up a story that the Queen had felt bitter remorse for the great crime by which she had obtained a throne, that in her agony she had applied to Tillotson, and that he had comforted her by assuring her that the punishment of the wicked in a future state would not be eternal.

"The Archbishop's mind was naturally of almost feminine delicacy, and had been rather softened than braced by the habits of a long life, during which contending sects and factions had agreed in speaking of his abilities with admiration and of his character with esteem. The storm of obloquy which he had to face for the first time at more than sixty years of age was too much for him. His spirits declined; his health gave way; yet he neither flinched from his duty nor attempted to revenge himself on his persecutors. A few days after his consecration, some persons were

MEMORABILIA.

seized while dispersing libels in which he was reviled.

"The law officers of the Crown proposed to institute prosecutions; but he insisted that nobody should be punished on his account. Once, when he had company with him a sealed packet was put into his hands: he opened it: and out fell a mask. His friends were shocked and incensed by this cowardly insult; but the Archbishop, trying to conceal his anguish by a smile, pointed to the pamphlets which covered his table, and said that the reproach which the emblem of mask was intended to convey might be called gentle when compared with other reproaches which he daily had to endure. After his death a bundle of the savage lampoons which the nonjurors had circulated against him was found among his papers with this endorsement: 'I pray God forgive them: I do.'"*

*Macaulay, History of England. Vol. iv. 29.

MEMORABILIA.

L'ENVOI.

Such are a few stray remembrances of this life which has been lived among us, this man sent from God who came to be a witness to the light that all men might believe.

The rest of life will be lonesome enough without him, but happy are they indeed who have seen and known and have been taught by the ministry of

PHILLIPS BROOKS.

www.ingramcontent.com/pod-product-compliance
Lightning Source LLC
Chambersburg PA
CBHW031121160426
43192CB00008B/1066